# MORE
# ANTONYMS

wild and tame and other
WORDS THAT ARE AS DIFFERENT
IN MEANING
as work and play

# MORE ANTONYMS

Joan Hanson

Published by
**Lerner Publications Company**
Minneapolis, Minnesota

FOR PAT !

**an·to·nym**   (AN-tuh-nim)   A word that means the opposite of another word. The antonym of *hard* is *soft*. *Tall* is the antonym of *short*.

**Hard**

**Soft**

**Plain**

Fancy

Dirty

**Clean**

**Lose**

**Find**

**Dark**

Light

**Old**

New

**Wild**

# Tame

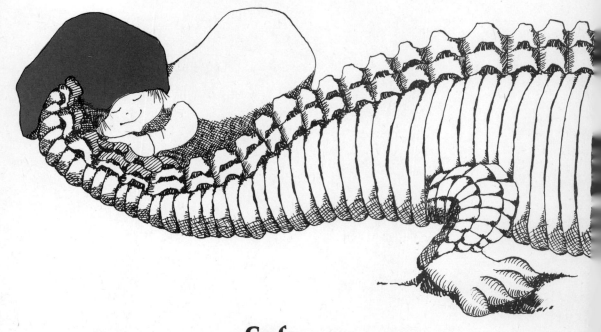

**Safe**

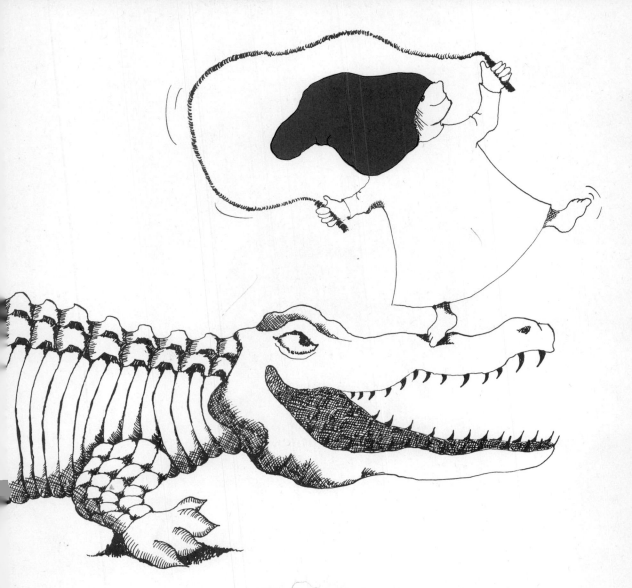

**Dangerous**

**Shallow**

**Deep**

**Graceful**

**Clumsy**

Work

**Play**

**Weak**

**Strong**

# BOOKS IN THIS SERIES

### ANTONYMS
hot and cold and other
WORDS THAT ARE DIFFERENT
as night and day

### MORE ANTONYMS
wild and tame and other
WORDS THAT ARE AS DIFFERENT IN MEANING
as work and play

### HOMONYMS
hair and hare and other
WORDS THAT SOUND THE SAME
but look as different as bear and bare

### MORE HOMONYMS
steak and stake and other
WORDS THAT SOUND THE SAME
but look as different as chili and chilly

### HOMOGRAPHS
bow and bow and other
WORDS THAT LOOK THE SAME
but sound as different as sow and sow

### HOMOGRAPHIC HOMOPHONES
fly and fly and other
WORDS THAT LOOK AND SOUND THE SAME
but are as different in meaning as bat and bat

### British-American SYNONYMS
french fries and chips and other
WORDS THAT MEAN THE SAME THING
but look and sound
as different as truck and lorry

### MORE SYNONYMS
shout and yell and other
WORDS THAT MEAN THE SAME THING
but look and sound
as different as loud and noisy

*We specialize in producing quality books for
young people. For a complete list please write*

## LERNER PUBLICATIONS COMPANY
241 First Avenue North, Minneapolis, Minnesota 55401